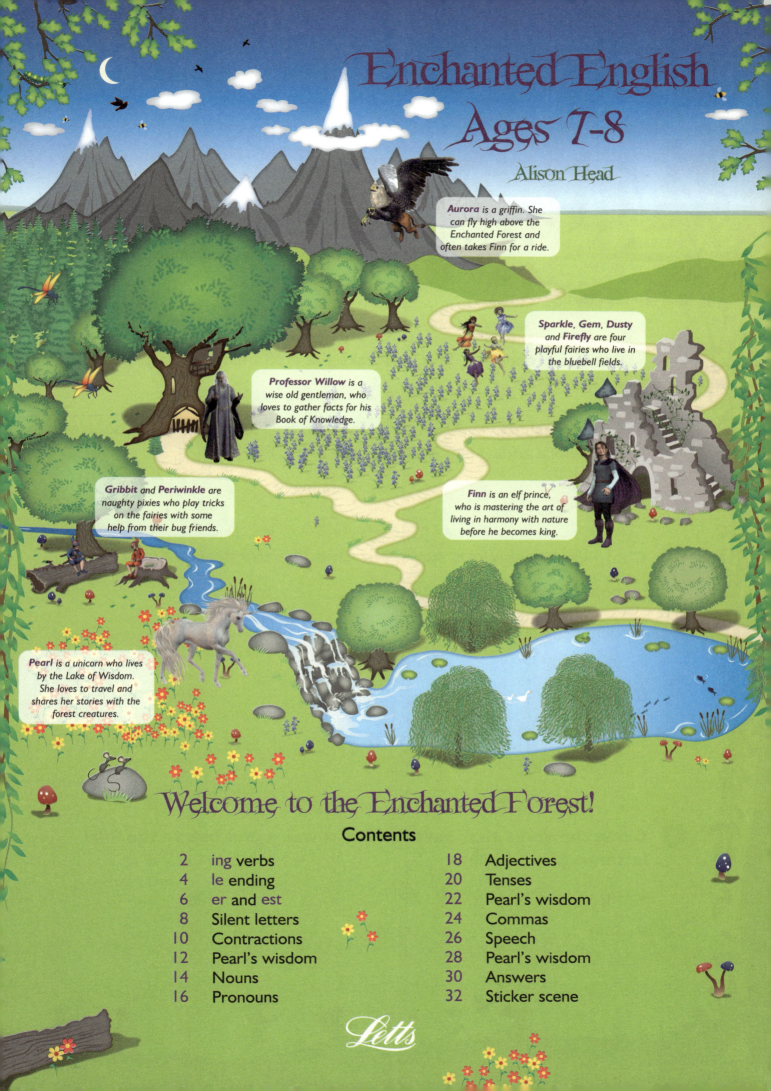

ing verbs

I'm Professor Willow and I'm here to teach you about verbs.

Verbs that end ing tell us what is happening right now.

fly   flying

If the verb ends in e, you must take the e off before adding ing.

make   making

If the verb has a short vowel sound before the final letter, you must double the final letter before adding ing. It's as easy as A-B-C!

run   running

1 Complete these word sums. No time like the present!

a hope + ing = _____

b take + ing = _____

c like + ing = _____

d give + ing = _____

e bite + ing = _____

f stroke + ing = _____

2 Circle the verbs that have a short vowel sound before the final letter, e.g. run, swim.

a tip   b go   c jog

d spin   e crawl   f fall

3 **Wonderful work! Now complete these word sums.**

a tap + ing = _____

b win + ing = _____

c slip + ing = _____

d fit + ing = _____

e shop + ing = _____

f flop + ing = _____

4 **Underline a mistake in each of these sentences, then write the correct word at the end.**

a The storm kept wakeing the fairies. _____

b The pixies are planing a grand ball. _____

c The baby rabbits were hideing in their burrow. _____

d It was begining to rain when Pearl set off on her journey. _____

e The young owls are learnning to fly. _____

f Sparkle practised balanceing on a blade of grass. _____

g Tiny silver fish were swimming in the pool. _____

Willow's Quest

Add ing to each of these verbs to complete the crossword grid.

a 1 across: dance

b 1 down: dive

c 2 down: sit

d 3 across: hit

e 4 across: bake

Now find the map at the back of the book and add the sticker of the frog.

le ending

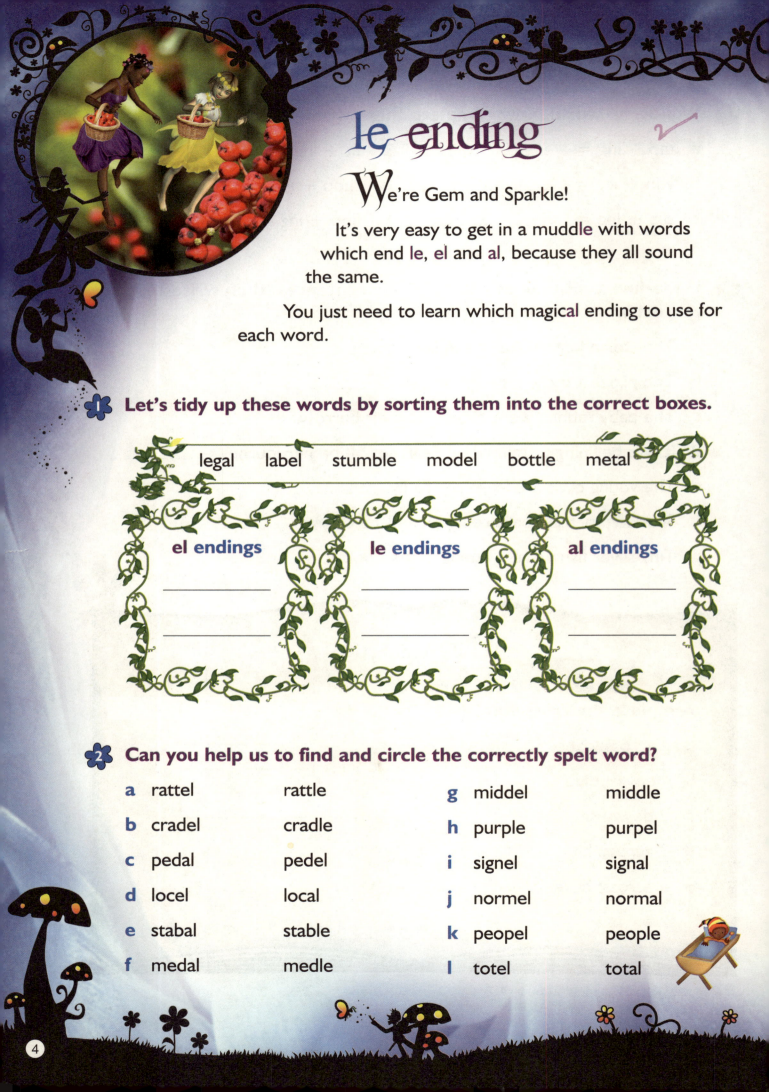

We're Gem and Sparkle!

It's very easy to get in a muddle with words which end le, el and al, because they all sound the same.

You just need to learn which magical ending to use for each word.

1 Let's tidy up these words by sorting them into the correct boxes.

legal   label   stumble   model   bottle   metal

el endings	le endings	al endings
_____	_____	_____
_____	_____	_____

2 Can you help us to find and circle the correctly spelt word?

a rattel   rattle   g middel   middle
b cradel   cradle   h purple   purpel
c pedal   pedel   i signel   signal
d locel   local   j normel   normal
e stabal   stable   k peopel   people
f medal   medle   l totel   total

3 **Dazzle us with your spelling skills! The pixies have spelt all of these words incorrectly. Can you write them again, with the correct spelling?**

a settel _____   e appel _____

b parcle _____   f muddel _____

c panle _____   g titel _____

d wobbel _____   h centrel _____

4 **Underline five spelling mistakes in this piece of text.**

It was time for the spring flower festivle in the Enchanted Forest. Fairies would travle for miles and each animal made sure their fur was brushed and their eyes were jewal-bright. Gribbit stood on a barral to get a better look. It tipped up and water spilt everywhere, leaving a huge puddel of water. What a muddle!

Willow's Quest

See if you can unscramble the letters to make five words which end with the le sound. Be careful – not all of the words end in the letters le!

a attleb _____   d agnel _____

b roaly _____   e eabl _____

c riplpe _____

Flit, flit! Pop the bluebells sticker on to the map.

er and est

My name is Pearl. Adjectives describe what things or people are like. Adding the suffix er or est to some adjectives can make them tell us even more.

    small   smaller   smallest

Sometimes you need to change the spelling of the root word first.

    pretty   prettier   safe   safest

See if you can complete these word sums. The Lake of Wisdom holds the answers!

a great + er = _____

b fast + est = _____

c late + er = _____

d close + est = _____

e funny + er = _____

f hot + est = _____

g big + er = _____

h lazy + est = _____

i brave + er = _____

j fine + est = _____

2 Underline the adjective in each sentence. Swish, swish!

a The oak is the tallest tree in the forest.

b Periwinkle is naughtier than Gribbit.

c Dusty is a quicker flier than Firefly.

d Professor Willow is the oldest person in the forest.

e The fairies prefer the brightest flowers.

3 Try writing your own sentences using these words. Take your time!

a warmer

_____

b silliest

_____

c loudest

_____

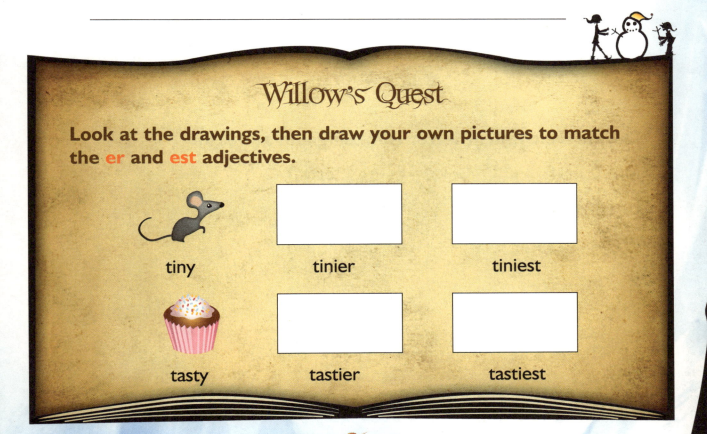

Willow's Quest

Look at the drawings, then draw your own pictures to match the er and est adjectives.

tiny   tinier   tiniest

tasty   tastier   tastiest

Add the unicorns sticker to the map.

Silent letters

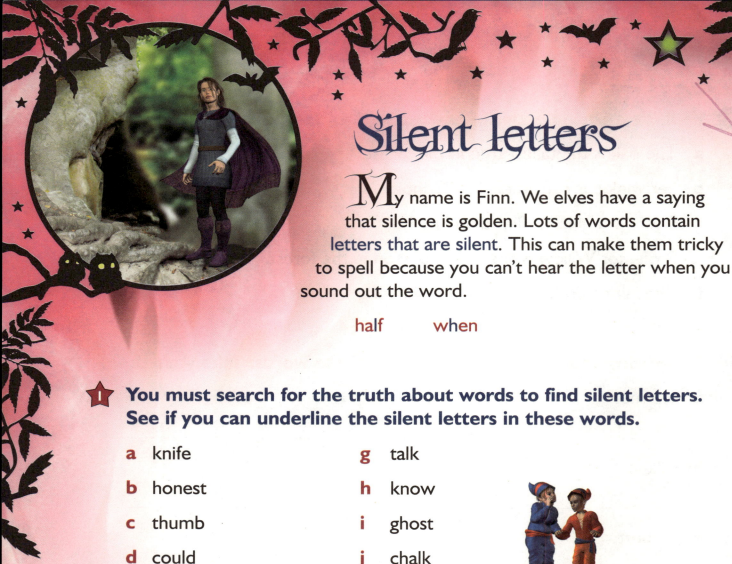

My name is Finn. We elves have a saying that silence is golden. Lots of words contain letters that are silent. This can make them tricky to spell because you can't hear the letter when you sound out the word.

half   when

1 You must search for the truth about words to find silent letters. See if you can underline the silent letters in these words.

a knife
b honest
c thumb
d could
e wrist
f climb

g talk
h know
i ghost
j chalk
k whisper
l wrong

2 Decide which silent letter is missing and add it in.

a ___night
b s___ord
c shou___d
d fo___k
e w___ich
f lam___

g c___orus
h ___rinkle
i ___rap
j si___n
k r___inoceros
l w___y

3 Now do these, word warrior. Try writing a sentence using each of these silent letter words.

a knot _____

b write _____

c knee _____

d chemist _____

e whistle _____

f design _____

Willow's Quest

Now that you have mastered silent letters, find these silent letter words in the word search.

a bomb
b debt
c gnome
d yolk
e knock

y	i	e	h	g
o	t	g	s	d
l	j	n	o	s
k	n	o	c	k
z	l	m	a	f
c	d	e	b	t
b	k	n	o	e
k	f	c	m	d
a	l	p	b	m

Find the owl sticker for your map.

Contractions

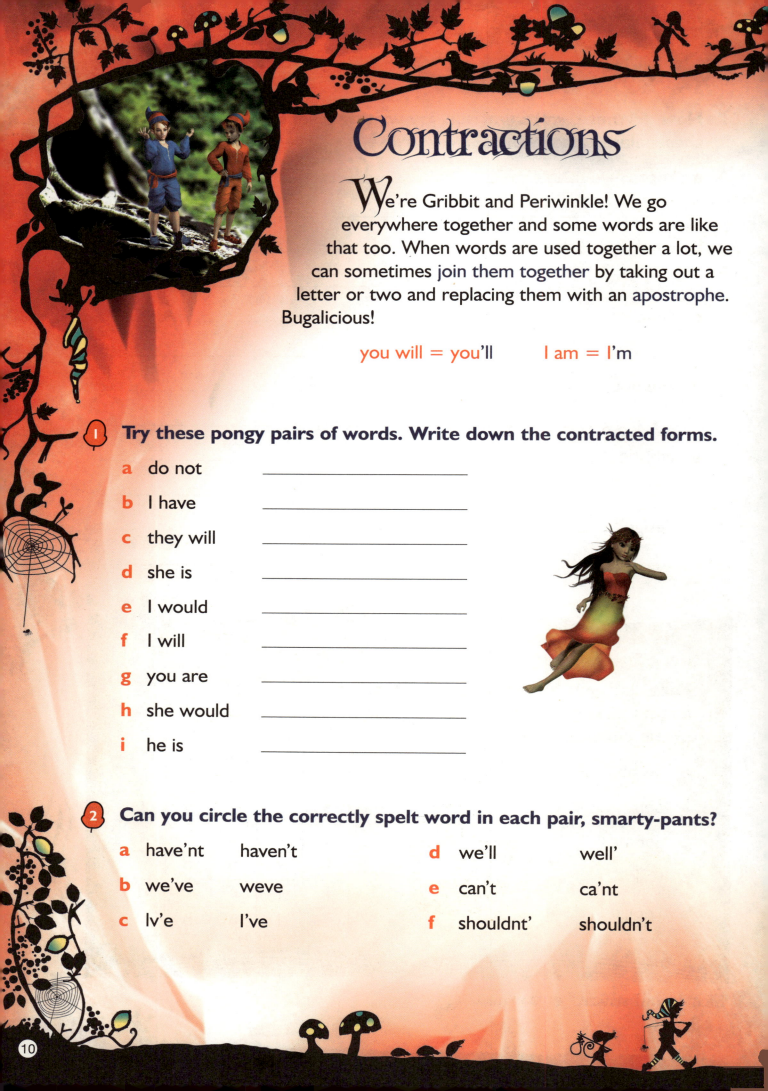

We're Gribbit and Periwinkle! We go everywhere together and some words are like that too. When words are used together a lot, we can sometimes join them together by taking out a letter or two and replacing them with an apostrophe. Bugalicious!

you will = you'll   I am = I'm

1 Try these pongy pairs of words. Write down the contracted forms.

a do not _____
b I have _____
c they will _____
d she is _____
e I would _____
f I will _____
g you are _____
h she would _____
i he is _____

2 Can you circle the correctly spelt word in each pair, smarty-pants?

a have'nt   haven't   d we'll   well'
b we've   weve   e can't   ca'nt
c Iv'e   I've   f shouldnt'   shouldn't

3 Have a go at rewriting these squelchy sentences, using the contracted forms of the bold words.

a When Finn has finished his book, **he will** read another one.

b Gem promised that **she would** play with Sparkle.

c Gribbit will eat after **he has** fired all of his arrows.

d **It will** be a beautiful night in the forest.

e **It is** magical by the Lake of Wisdom.

Willow's Quest

Lots of contracted words contain the word not, to make the opposite meaning.

For example, should becomes shouldn't. We have borrowed Professor Willow's opposites machine to add not to these words.

a could

b is   IN   OUT

c will

d are

e shall

Add the mice sticker to your map.

Pearl's wisdom

1 Look carefully at these sentences. Can you write the sentences again with the word in bold spelt correctly? Take your time!

a Aurora rose into the air, **flaping** her wings.

_____

b The pixies spoke to the animals **liveing** in the tree.

_____

c The baby rabbits love **hoping** about in the forest.

_____

2 Underline the word in each sentence that ends with the **le** sound. Remember, the endings may be spelt differently!

a Gem hopped on to a large, pink flower petal.

b Periwinkle and Gribbit don't like people visiting the Enchanted Forest.

c A little mouse ran into the bracken.

d The pixies have a table made out of twigs.

3 Use the magic within you to complete the table.

	root word	+ er	+ est
a	fine	finer	
b	young		youngest
c	bright	brighter	
d	silly		silliest
e	happy	happier	

4 Circle the words which contain silent letters.

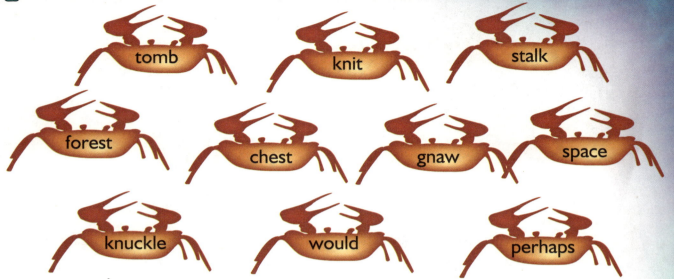

tomb   knit   stalk   forest   chest   gnaw   space   knuckle   would   perhaps

5 Write sentences using the contracted form of these words.

a I will _____

b we are _____

c it will _____

d he would _____

6 Underline the correctly spelt word from each pair to complete these sentences.

a The fairies are (takeing/taking) a picnic to eat by the Lake of Wisdom.

b Gribbit and Periwinkle sent smoke (signels/signals) across the forest to each other.

c Sparkle drew a hopscotch grid on the ground with (chalk/chahk).

d The pixies argued about which of them was (hungryer/hungrier).

e Professor Willow (wo'nt/won't) be back until later.

f Finn used a (knotted/notted) rope to climb the tree.

Add the crystals sticker to the map.

Nouns

Nouns are words that name things, like rabbits, foxes and trees.

Nouns are special because they can be singular or plural. Singular means one and plural means two or more. Many plurals end s, but nouns which end in a hissing, buzzing or shushing sound end es.

add s ➔ acorn**s**   add es ➔ dish**es**

1 Circle the nouns in this group of words. No time like the present!

- slowly
- bag
- candle
- happy
- huge
- apple
- red
- mouse
- pencil
- door

2 Now underline the plural noun in each sentence.

a Professor Willow owns many books.

b Aurora collects interesting objects in her nest.

c Gribbit and Periwinkle hide among the bushes.

d The animals of the forest gathered to hear Pearl sing.

e Sparkle and Dusty live in the flowers.

f Squirrels leapt from branch to branch.

3 Wonderful work! Can you circle the correct plural for each of these singular nouns?

a fox | foxes | foxs
b house | houses | housees
c watch | watchs | watches
d plant | plants | plantes
e car | cares | cars
f ash | ashs | ashes

4 Complete each sentence with the plural of the bold word at the end.

a Pearl granted Gem three _____. **wish**

b Sparkle sewed _____ on to Gribbit's torn shirt. **patch**

c Harvest mice live in tiny _____ made from straw. **nest**

d The magical fruit tree grows cherries, apples and _____. **peach**

e The forest _____ gathered for the party. **creature**

Willow's Quest

Can you write down the plurals for these words?

a glass _____
b key _____
c kiss _____
d table _____
e sandwich _____

Add the Book of Knowledge sticker to the map.

Pronouns

My name is Aurora. Pronouns are words that we can often use instead of a noun. They save us from having to use the same noun over and over again, which makes our writing more interesting.

Professor Willow has many books because he loves to read.

1 See if you can underline the pronoun in each sentence.

a Because she loves showing off, Dusty flew above the clouds.

b Pearl asked Gribbit and Periwinkle where they were going.

c We must be quiet in the Enchanted Forest.

d As Pearl sang, butterflies fluttered around her.

e The Book of Knowledge is magical because it contains many secrets.

2 You're flying through this! Circle the correct pronoun from the brackets to complete each sentence.

a Gem is angry with the pixies because (she they we) played a trick on her.

b Pearl asked Professor Willow if (us she we) could look in the Book of Knowledge.

c Finn lives in the forest because (they he us) is preparing to be king.

d When the forest creatures left the glade, Finn followed (we you them).

e Firefly was thrilled when Dusty gave (me her him) a beautiful flower.

f Gribbit hid among the trees and Periwinkle tried to find (it her him).

3 **The sky is the limit with pronouns! Write these sentences again, using a pronoun in place of the bold words.**

a When the hedgehog saw the fox, **the hedgehog** curled into a tight ball.

_____

_____

b Realising **Professor Willow** was late, Professor Willow hurried out of the door.

_____

_____

c Gribbit and Periwinkle make their furniture out of acorns **Gribbit and Periwinkle** find in the forest.

_____

_____

Willow's Quest

Choose a pronoun, which you could use to replace each of these nouns. Then add another pronoun of your own for each one.

we   him   them   she

a Dusty and Sparkle   _____   _____
b Professor Willow   _____   _____
c Aurora   _____   _____
d you and your friends _____   _____

Pop the sticker of the flock of birds on your map.

Adjectives

Adjectives are words that describe nouns. You must choose them carefully to help your reader imagine what people, places and things are like.

a brilliant idea   a spooky castle   the heroic knight

1 **Let's get busy! Circle the adjective in each sentence.**

a The fairies played among the colourful flowers.
b Gribbit began to climb the tallest tree in the forest.
c The bird's nest was an untidy collection of twigs.
d The Lake of Wisdom was blue in the moonlight.
e Pearl told the fairies an exciting story.
f Professor Willow has a collection of ancient books.

2 **Draw a line to match up each noun with a sensible adjective to describe it.**

a the wind   crispy
b the sand   spiky
c an acorn   golden
d autumn leaves   gusty
e brambles   shiny

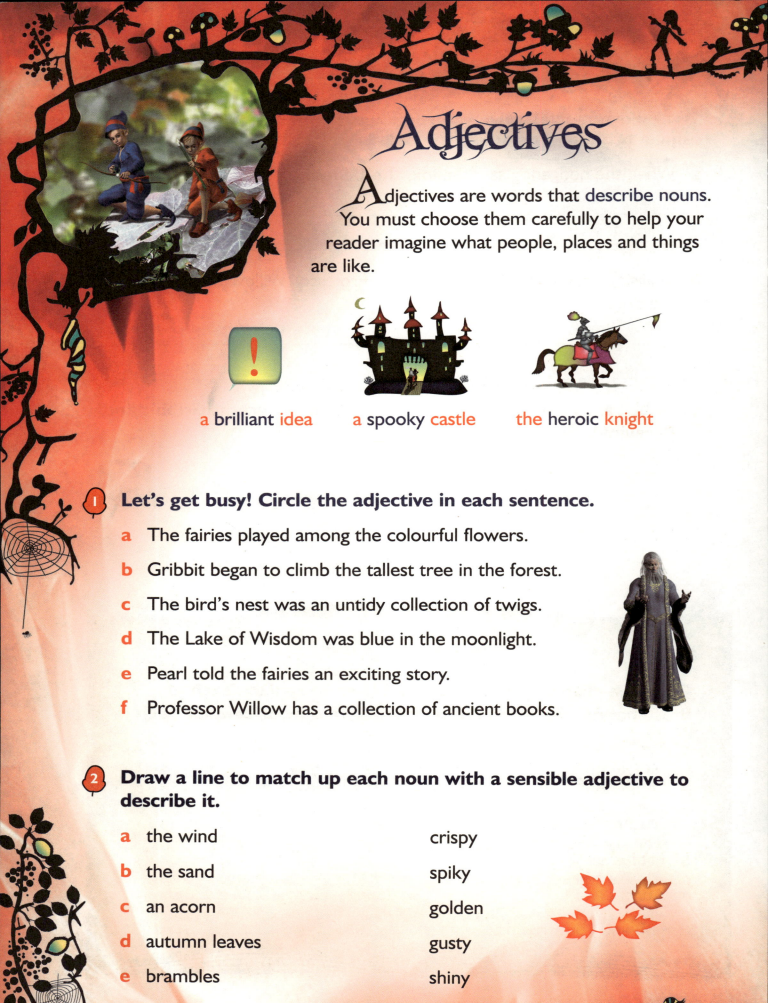

3 Write down an adjective you could use to describe each of these nouns. Bugalicious!

a a _____ butterfly

b the _____ moon

c a _____ fox

d a _____ mountain

e _____ clouds

4 Write a sentence using each of these adjectives.

a crunchy _____

b mysterious _____

c creepy _____

d precious _____

e fragile _____

Willow's Quest

Adjectives like **big** or **nice** can be very boring. Cross out the boring adjective in the brackets in each of these sentences.

a Professor Willow has a (big/huge) collection of books.

b Gem and Firefly were (furious/cross) with Gribbit and Periwinkle.

c The moles make a (bad/terrible) mess with their molehills.

d A (beautiful/nice) rainbow appeared over the Enchanted Forest.

e A (small/tiny) beetle scurried away.

Pop the woodland picnic sticker on the map.

Tenses

Balance is the key to understanding verb tenses. Past tense verbs tell us about something that happened in the past. They often end ed.

talk   talked

Other past tense verbs are spelt differently. We need to learn them carefully.

sleep   slept

1 Draw lines to match up the pairs of present tense and past tense verbs.

a say   was
b buy   heard
c hear   rode
d go   bought
e am   went
f ride   said

2 Now try these, word warrior. Underline the correct past tense verb from each pair.

a eat   eated   ate
b swim   swimmed   swam
c know   knowed   knew
d draw   drew   drawed
e grow   growed   grew
f keep   kept   keeped

3 **Now write a sentence using each of these past tense verbs.**

a caught _____

b threw _____

c learnt _____

d flew _____

e wrote _____

f ran _____

4 **Look at the verb to help you decide whether these sentences are written in the present tense or the past tense. Write PRESENT or PAST at the end of each one.**

a Professor Willow thought carefully about the problem. _____

b Sparkle and Firefly giggle when they hear a funny joke. _____

c Many of the trees in the Enchanted Forest are very old. _____

d The fairies danced in the moonlight. _____

e Gribbit and Periwinkle ate all of the blackberries. _____

Willow's Quest

Look at these magical verbs in the Book of Knowledge. Colour the present tense verbs red and the past tense verbs green.

teach   liked   made

found   make   find

taught   like

Add the treasure chest sticker to the map.

Pearl's wisdom

1 Use the magic within you to write down the plural form of these nouns.

a witch _____
b box _____
c wish _____
d pitch _____
e castle _____

f stick _____
g match _____
h trolley _____
i tassel _____
j alley _____

2 Now add a pronoun to complete each sentence.

a When Gribbit and Periwinkle had finished exploring, _____ went home.

b Finn lives in a cave when _____ visits the forest.

c Gem rested on a flower because _____ was tired.

d "Can _____ sit down too?" asked Sparkle and Firefly.

e The rabbit bounded away because _____ was afraid.

f Goblins came into the Enchanted Forest, so the pixies chased _____ away.

g When Professor Willow is working, nobody must disturb _____ .

h The animals gathered around Pearl to hear _____ sing.

3 Write down a more interesting adjective that you could use instead of each of these. Take your time!

a nice _____   e cold _____

b kind _____   f old _____

c fast _____   g funny _____

d hot _____   h dirty _____

4 Look carefully at these present tense verbs. Can you sort them into verbs that end ed in the past tense and those which have irregular past tense endings?

wish   shout   hide   weep   look   is   climb   drive

regular ed ending   irregular past tense ending

5 Write these sentences again, in the past tense.

a The fairies go ice skating in the winter.

_____

b Pearl wonders what the mountains are like.

_____

c The squirrels collect nuts for the winter.

_____

d Pearl sings a song for the animals.

_____

e Professor Willow tidies his bookshelves.

_____

Add the shells sticker to the map.

Commas

Commas are useful for separating items in lists. We also use them to help our readers understand our sentences. We can put in a comma to show our readers when to take a **short pause** when they are reading.

Late in the evening, it began to rain.

1 **Add a comma to one of the spaces in each sentence.**

a Laughing quietly Gribbit and Periwinkle hid from the fairies.

b Because they are so tiny the fairies can hide among the flowers.

c The fairies scattered pink, blue green and purple fairy dust.

d When Pearl reached the clearing she began to sing beautifully.

e Foxes rabbits and badgers live in burrows among the trees.

f The pixies make their furniture from things they find like twigs and acorns.

2 **The sky is the limit with sentences! See if you can think of a sensible way to end each of these sentences.**

a Flying over the Lake of Wisdom, _____.

b When humans visit the forest, _____.

c Aurora collects unusual treasures, _____.

d Because unicorns are magical, _____.

e Sparkle, Dusty, Gem and Firefly _____.

3 **You're flying through this! Draw lines between pairs of phrases to make sensible sentences.**

a   When the moon rose,   Professor Willow took his umbrella.

b   Before he can be king,   Aurora takes messages to the elf palace.

c   The fairies will be angry, Finn must spend time in the Enchanted Forest.

d   When they see that winter is on the way,   it cast beautiful shadows in the forest.

e   Noticing that it was raining,   if the pixies play another trick on them.

f   Because she can fly,   the squirrels start to gather nuts.

g   While Professor Willow is working,   so the animals gathered round to listen.

h   Pearl was telling a story,   the fairies must play quietly.

Willow's Quest

You're a star! Read these sentences carefully and decide which ones have commas in the correct place. Put a tick in the box beside them.

a   While looking for acorns, the pixies found a magic crystal.

b   While, they waited for the sun to rise the fairies played hide-and-seek.

c   Some of the trees in the forest are so tall, even the pixies can't climb to the top.

d   Startled by the sound of voices, the deer leapt away.

e   Because Pearl has travelled to so many places she has great, stories to tell.

Add the hedgehogs sticker to your map.

Speech

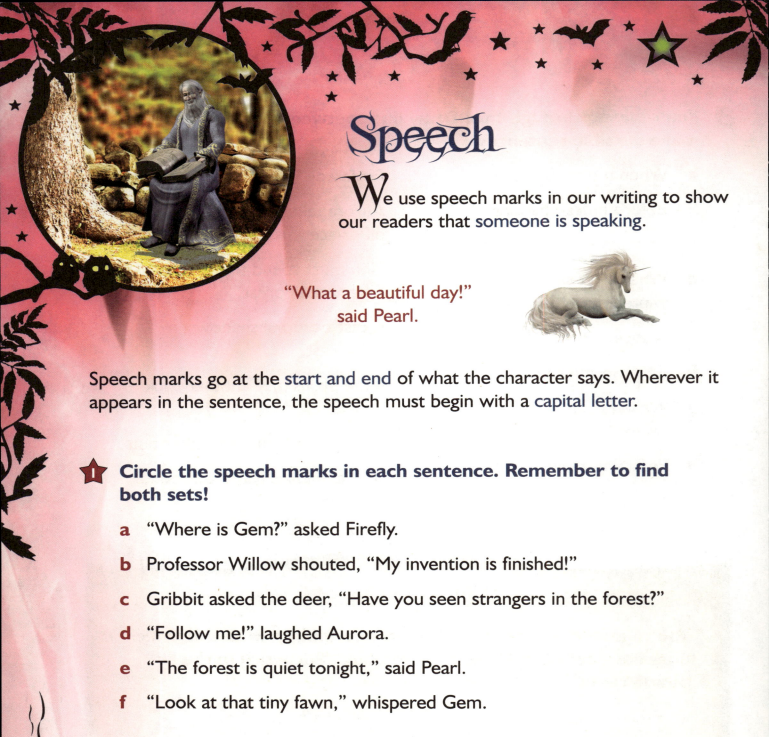

We use speech marks in our writing to show our readers that someone is speaking.

"What a beautiful day!" said Pearl.

Speech marks go at the start and end of what the character says. Wherever it appears in the sentence, the speech must begin with a capital letter.

1 **Circle the speech marks in each sentence. Remember to find both sets!**

a "Where is Gem?" asked Firefly.

b Professor Willow shouted, "My invention is finished!"

c Gribbit asked the deer, "Have you seen strangers in the forest?"

d "Follow me!" laughed Aurora.

e "The forest is quiet tonight," said Pearl.

f "Look at that tiny fawn," whispered Gem.

2 **Wounderful work! Now add the speech marks to these sentences. There are gaps there for you.**

a When will the Professor be back? asked the pixies.

b Aurora said, The unicorns are playing by the lake.

c Shall I tell you a story? asked Pearl.

d Finn explained, Focus is very important in learning.

e Periwinkle whispered, There are humans in the forest!

3 Read this conversation to see who is saying what. Then write the name of each speaker and what they say in the speech bubbles. You do not need speech marks in speech bubbles.

"Have you seen the pixies?" asked Pearl. "Yes, they are by the Lake of Wisdom," said Professor Willow. "I need them to play music for me," explained Pearl. "We all love your singing!" exclaimed Professor Willow.

Willow's Quest

Use the words in the speech bubbles to help you add speech to these sentences. Make sure you put the speech marks in the correct places and remember the capital letter!

- What a wonderful idea!
- I have seen some amazing places.
- The elf palace is beautiful.

a _____, said Professor Willow.

b Pearl exclaimed, _____.

c _____, declared Finn.

Add the rabbit and squirrel sticker to the map.

Pearl's wisdom

1 **Here is a story about one of my adventures. Read it carefully and think about the sentences. Underline any sentences that you think would be easier to read if they included a comma. Now write the passage again, with the commas in place. Just do your best!**

I decided to travel beyond the Enchanted Forest to look for the Crystal Cave which lies far to the north. I had heard from a passing pixie that it contains thousands of beautiful crystals sparkling in the sunlight. Crossing a raging river I saw the cave ahead. It was amazing. It shimmered in the light like a huge diamond set high in the cliff face. I couldn't wait to see inside. I climbed the cliff and peered inside. Inside every surface was covered with tiny crystals. They bounced rainbow patterns across the floor of the cave in all directions. I will never forget it.

2 **Look carefully at the text below. Use the magic within you to write this story in your own words. Include what the characters say, with speech marks.**

Gem came zooming into Pearl's forest glade, panting. She explained quickly that Firefly had flown too close to a bramble bush and her wings were tangled in the prickles.

Pearl reassured Gem that everything was going to be alright and told her to fetch Finn and take him to the bramble bush. When Gem told Finn what had happened, he ran to help and gently eased Firefly's wings out of trouble.

When he had finished, Firefly declared that she felt much better and fluttered around Finn to prove it!

Finish your map by adding the dragonflies sticker.

Answers

Pages 2–3
1. a hoping d giving
   b taking e biting
   c liking f stroking
2. The verbs that should be circled are:
   a) tip, c) jog and d) spin.
3. a tapping d fitting
   b winning e shopping
   c slipping f flopping
4. a waking e learning
   b planning f balancing
   c hiding g swimming
   d beginning

Willow's Quest

Pages 4–5
1. el endings: label, model
   le endings: stumble, bottle
   al endings: legal, metal
2. The correctly spelt words are:
   a rattle g middle
   b cradle h purple
   c pedal i signal
   d local j normal
   e stable k people
   f medal l total
3. a settle e apple
   b parcel f muddle
   c panel g title
   d wobble h central
4. It was time for the spring flower festivle in the Enchanted Forest. Fairies would travle for miles and each animal made sure their fur was brushed and their eyes were jewal-bright. Gribbit stood on a barral to get a better look. It tipped up and water spilt everywhere, leaving a huge puddel of water. What a muddle!

Willow's Quest
a battle d angel or angle
b royal e able
c ripple

Pages 6–7
1. a greater g bigger
   b fastest h laziest
   c later i braver
   d closest j finest
   e funnier k bolder
   f hottest
2. a tallest
   b naughtier
   c quicker
   d oldest
   e brightest
3. Sentences will vary.

Willow's Quest
Pictures will vary.

Pages 8–9
1. a knife g talk
   b honest h know
   c thumb i ghost
   d could j chalk
   e wrist k whisper
   f climb l wrong
2. a knight g chorus
   b sword h wrinkle
   c should i wrap
   d folk j sign
   e which k rhinoceros
   f lamb l why
3. Sentences will vary.

Willow's Quest

y	l	e	h	g
o	t	g	s	d
l	j	n	o	s
k	n	o	c	k
z	l	m	a	f
c	d	e	b	t
b	k	n	o	e
k	f	c	m	d
a	l	p	b	m

Pages 10–11
1. a don't f I'll
   b I've g you're
   c they'll h she'd
   d she's i he's
   e I'd
2. a haven't d we'll
   b we've e can't
   c I've f shouldn't
3. a When Finn has finished his book, he'll read another one.
   b Gem promised that she'd play with Sparkle.
   c Gribbit will eat after he's fired all of his arrows.
   d It'll be a beautiful night in the forest.
   e It's magical by the Lake of Wisdom.

Willow's Quest
a couldn't d aren't
b isn't e shan't
c won't

Pages 12–13
Pearl's Wisdom
1. Sentences will vary, but should include the following words:
   a flapping
   b living
   c hopping
2. a Gem hopped on to a large, pink flower petal.
   b Periwinkle and Gribbit don't like people visiting the Enchanted Forest.
   c A little mouse ran into the bracken.
   d The pixies have a table made out of twigs.
3.

root word	+ er	+ est
a fine	finer	finest
b young	younger	youngest
c bright	brighter	brightest
d silly	sillier	silliest
e happy	happier	happiest

4. The words which contain silent letters are: tomb, stalk, knuckle, gnaw, would, knit.
5. Sentences will vary, but should include the following contractions:
   a I'll c it'll
   b we're d he'd
6. a taking d hungrier
   b signals e won't
   c chalk f knotted

Pages 14–15
1. The nouns are: bag, candle, mouse, apple, door, pencil.
2. a Professor Willow owns many books.
   b Aurora collects interesting objects in her nest.
   c Gribbit and Periwinkle hide among the bushes.
   d The animals of the forest gathered to hear Pearl sing.
   e Sparkle and Dusty live in the flowers.
   f Squirrels leapt from branch to branch.
3. a foxes d plants
   b houses e cars
   c watches f ashes
4. a wishes d peaches
   b patches e creatures
   c nests

Willow's Quest
a glasses d tables
b keys e sandwiches
c kisses

Pages 16–17
1 a Because <u>she</u> loves showing off, Dusty flew above the clouds.
  b Pearl asked Gribbit and Periwinkle where <u>they</u> were going.
  c <u>We</u> must be quiet in the Enchanted Forest.
  d As Pearl sang, butterflies fluttered around <u>her</u>.
  e The Book of Knowledge is magical because <u>it</u> contains many secrets.
2 a they   d them
  b she   e her
  c he   f him
3 a When the hedgehog saw the fox, it curled into a tight ball.
  b Realising he was late, Professor Willow hurried out of the door.
  c Gribbit and Periwinkle make their furniture out of acorns they find in the forest.

Willow's Quest
  a them   they
  b him   he
  c she   her
  d we   us

Pages 18–19
1 a colourful   d blue
  b tallest   e exciting
  c untidy   f ancient
2 a the wind   crispy
  b the sand   spiky
  c an acorn   golden
  d autumn leaves   gusty
  e brambles   shiny
3 Answers will vary, but might include:
  a colourful   d huge
  b pale   e fluffy
  c crafty
4 Sentences will vary.

Willow's Quest
The boring adjectives are:
a big   d nice
b cross   e small
c bad

Pages 20–21
Tenses
1 a say   was
  b buy   heard
  c hear   rode
  d go   bought
  e am   went
  f ride   said
2 a ate   d drew
  b swam   e grew
  c knew   f kept
3 Sentences will vary.
4 a PAST   d PAST
  b PRESENT   e PAST
  c PRESENT

Willow's Quest
Present tense verbs should be coloured in red: teach, make, find, like.
Past tense verbs should be coloured in green: taught, made, found, liked.

Pages 22–23
Pearl's Wisdom
1 a witches   f sticks
  b boxes   g matches
  c wishes   h trolleys
  d pitches   i tassels
  e castles   j alleys
2 a they   e it
  b he   f them
  c she   g him
  d we   h her
3 Answers will vary, but might include:
  a friendly   e freezing
  b generous   f ancient
  c speedy   g hilarious
  d boiling   h grimy
4 ed ending: wish, shout, look, climb
  irregular past tense ending: hide, weep, is, drive
5 a The fairies went ice skating in the winter.
  b Pearl wondered what the mountains were like.
  c The squirrels collected nuts for the winter.
  d Pearl sang a song for the animals.
  e Professor Willow tidied his bookshelves.

Pages 24–25
1 a Laughing quietly, Gribbit and Periwinkle hid from the fairies.
  b Because they are so tiny, the fairies can hide among the flowers.
  c The fairies scattered pink, blue, green and purple fairy dust.
  d When Pearl reached the clearing, she began to sing beautifully.
  e Foxes, rabbits and badgers live in burrows among the trees.
  f The pixies make their furniture from things they find, like twigs and acorns.
2 Answers will vary.
3 a When the moon rose, it cast beautiful shadows in the forest.
  b Before he can be king, Finn must spend time in the Enchanted Forest.
  c The fairies will be angry, if the pixies play another trick on them.
  d When they see that winter is on the way, the squirrels start to gather nuts.
  e Noticing that it was raining, Professor Willow took his umbrella.
  f Because she can fly, Aurora takes messages to the elf palace.
  g While Professor Willow is working, the fairies must play quietly.
  h Pearl was telling a story, so the animals gathered round to listen.

Willow's Quest
The correct sentences are: a, c and d.

Pages 26–27
1 a "Where is Gem?" asked Firefly.
  b Professor Willow shouted, "My invention is finished!"
  c Gribbit asked the deer, "Have you seen strangers in the forest?"
  d "Follow me!" laughed Aurora.
  e "The forest is quiet tonight," said Pearl.
  f "Look at that tiny fawn," whispered Gem.
2 a "When will the Professor be back?" asked the pixies.
  b Aurora said, "The unicorns are playing by the lake".
  c "Shall I tell you a story?" asked Pearl.
  d Finn explained, "Focus is very important in learning."
  e Periwinkle whispered, "There are humans in the forest!"
3

Have you seen the pixies? — Pearl
Yes, they are by the Lake of Wisdom, — Professor Willow
I need them to play music for me. — Pearl
We all love your singing! — Professor Willow

Willow's Quest
a "What a wonderful idea!" said Professor Willow.
b Pearl exclaimed, "I have seen some amazing places."
c "The elf palace is beautiful," declared Finn.

Pages 28–29
Pearl's Wisdom
1 The position of the commas may vary, but commas should be used appropriately to aid understanding of the text. Possible answers include:
I decided to travel beyond the Enchanted Forest to look for the Crystal Cave, which lies to the north. I had heard from a passing pixie, that it contains thousands of beautiful crystals, sparkling in the sunlight. Crossing a raging river, I saw the cave ahead. It was amazing. It shimmered in the light like a huge diamond, set high in the cliff face. I couldn't wait to see inside. I climbed the cliff and peered inside. Inside, every surface was covered with tiny crystals. They bounced rainbow patterns across the floor of the cave, in all directions. I will never forget it.
2 Answers will vary, but the sentences should explain how Finn helps Firefly and Gem. Speech marks should be in the correct places.

Enchanted Forest Map Stickers

Extra Stickers